Hold on, Let go

GW00470415

Gemma Herbertson

BookLeaf Publishing

Hold on, Let go © 2022 Gemma Herbertson

Presentation by *BookLeaf Publishing*

Web: www.bookleafpub.com

E-mail: info@bookleafpub.com

ISBN: 9789357617451

First edition 2022

I dedicate this book to my daughter, Freya Herbertson-Hill, for being my constant inspiration and source of great pride, and for always believing in me.

ACKNOWLEDGEMENT

Hold on, I think this is my chance to let go...yes, here's the gushy bit, and there are some very special people who deserve a mention here for their role in the blossoming of this book.

I would very much like to thank and acknowledge the team at Book Leaf Publishing without whom I would not have got this collection out into the world. I am particularly grateful for the deadline they gave – it really helps! I am also indebted to Mark Hide for giving me the wake-up prep-talk and kick up the backside I needed to get this done. I am very blessed to have my wonderful friend Ruth Bennett, who always keeps me feeling positive with an 'I can do this' attitude. I must also mention Barry Hitchcock MBE RIP, a wonderful man, and the best boss I ever had, and who made a very timely appearance in a dream during this project, reminding me to always do my best in life.

I must also thank Dr Iain McGilchrist for teaching me how life is simultaneously individual elements and interconnectedness - a concept perfectly depicted by the "Indra's Net" concept (such a penny dropping analogy – I urge you to look it up if you have not come across it before). Earlier this year, alongside Satish Kumar, Iain led a lovely poetry sharing session at the wonderful Schumacher College, which expanded my appreciation of how many secret poetry lovers are quietly out there. I must also thank Satish Kumar for his inspiring words about the need to let go: many times we over-complicate life, when simplicity is often so much better. Thank you, Satish.

I would like to express thanks to Dr Simon Robinson, for introducing me to the world of public poetry; and I must also pay tribute to my local poetry group, Poetika, in Salisbury, for tolerantly allowing me to stand on their monthly stage and read out some semblance of sensical, and often non-sensical, words. I am humbled and inspired by the ears and voices of those who attend, and who even politely clap at the end. This is a vulnerable and valuable experience, which has definitely helped me to build some confidence in my words.

Within my family, I must thank my father for his support; and also say a huge thank you to my two fun and fabulous children, Freya and Eddy, for giving me my best reason to get up each day and to do projects like this one. You are both great!

PREFACE

The Serenity Prayer
God, grant me the serenity to
accept the things I cannot change,
the courage to change the things I can,
and the wisdom to know the difference
       Prof. Reinhold Niebuhr

Ever the optimist, I like to wear my best smile and my favourite coat – the one with the silver lining. I also eat my eggs sunny side up and look for the joy in everything. However, life continues to teach me that one of Newton's laws of physics rings as true in life as it does in science, and that for every action in nature there is an equal and opposite reaction. So, when life is rosy, it calls for humbleness, and when life throws lemons, shout "Carpe diem!" and squeeze the day!

This collection of poems has been a way for me to share some of the actions and reactions I observe in life – from the brightest highs to their lacklustre lows (and some of the various hues in-between). I hope you will enjoy what you read and find your own meanings and insight from amongst the words.

And, if you are wondering about me and my relationship with arranging and rearranging just 26 letters, well, poetry has been a part of my life for over twenty years, and I love to use it to condense and distil, as well as expand and clarify my thoughts and ideas. It is very cathartic to me, and I also love the feeling of accomplishment (and my audible sigh of contentment) when I have got a poem 'just so' – often very much the result of 'courageous' decisions of when to hold on and when to let go of a word or a line.

And, although I have been writing for pleasure for many years, this is the first time I have been bold enough to put some of these words into an actual book. I also want to share how I am always amazed by how life turns out, as putting together this collection happened via a happy piece of serendipity and collision of events: During a beautiful walk around the Uffington White Horse (a huge and prehistoric chalk hillside figure) a friend challenged me to find the time to write a book, and the next day, just as I had carved out a five-day window to focus on this, I found out about a 'write your book' series of workshops happening in those exact five days, and I ALSO heard about a wonderful poetry challenge to be started that week! Wowee - the stars certainly felt as if they were aligning! Suddenly, I had the time, the tools, and the motivation, and so I made the commitment! And now I am very grateful that you are reading this book, and I very much hope that the words will give you something back in return for your time and effort in reading them.

In gratitude.

Threads of Gold

Threads of gold between them flow,
Reaching out,
Their spirits glow.

Beacons, drawing each one in.
Magnetic force,
Its source within.

His voice it turns her inside out
Want to give?
Without a doubt.

Every word a masterpiece.
Fall her body
To her knees.

He pours a glass of happiness.
She's full
Desires
She's lost
She's his.

And all the while, soft as a sigh,
Felt him coming,
Not know why.

Like the One,
A special sign.
A presence bright,
Intense - it shines!

Feelings now (once kept within)
Leaking out
It's him,
It's him!

And every day these feelings rise,
Strong, defenceless,
Grounded, highs.

Questions, answers from his soul.
Unlock her joy
And make her whole.

Open now. Oh - please, come in!
Turn the key
Begin,
Begin!

Hold her close - feel her heart.
New. Familiar.
The end. The start.

Electric, soothing,
Secret, bold.
A promise remembered.
It's new. It's old.

Then she turns to look again:
Benedictus
Hominem

Time was waiting: meant to be.
Caught by him,
Yet, never more free.

Secrets

Close, so close
Feel the barrier:
There!
Seems invisible
Made of air.

Barometric pressure on the rise
Don't let them in!
Keep the disguise

Old storms weathered
New guards in place
Noone can guess.
Such a perfect face.

A strong harbour wall
The secrets are safe
No boat will ever
Leave this place

Everything accounted for
Nothing to deliver
A life in order
Don't stop to consider.

Ho! - Where's the joy?
I fear only pain
Yet there can't be rainbows
Without the rain.

But sunbeams await
Beyond the walls
See the horizon
Be gone you fools!

So, unfurl your sails
And let the winds in
Trust where they blow you
And no end can begin.

Into Your Arms

Into your arms:
A soothing balm.
Secure and safe.
Relief and calm.

This space: it's ours –
A vacuum, a pocket.
Where time stands still,
All worries unknotted.

And in this pause,
From the business of life,
Love melts all tension,
As warmth melts ice.

Rendered defenceless,
Vulnerable, free.
Your arms enable
No airs: true me.

Intertwined.
A perfect knit.
Touching. Soothing.
A benefit.

Feeling now,
Bodies aglow,
Hearts beat gently,
A love a-flow.

The Lighthouse

Darkest night
Screaming winds
Scaling waves
No end begins

Engine room
Hot. No air.
Give us power
Take her there

Coming now
Heavy wave
Eyes await
Hearts are brave

Holding on
No time to think
Hold her steady
Lest we sink

Driving, driving
All her might
In God's Hands
Hold on tight

Vertical
Reach the top
Sudden level
No time to stop

Falling now
Up ahead
Flash of light
Marks their beds

The Lighthouse
Standing
On the hill
The Lighthouse
Beaming
Out God's Will

Beacon gone
Black of night
Sweating hands
Feel their plight

Crashing down
Sliding feet
A jolt. A stall.
Yet not defeat

For there He is
Standing still
Hopeful pillar
Even keel

The Lighthouse
Standing
On the hill
The Lighthouse
Beaming
Out God's Will

Calling them:
Persist. Persist.
Homeward bound
Desist. Desist.

Moment of light
As a spark
Signals safety
From the dark

Though they have
No way of knowing
Guiding Light
Forever showing

Darkness marks
Time of thinking
Darkness marks
Fear of sinking

Slowly turning
Process pain
Hearts yearning
Sight again

Open eyes
Raising hopes
Light returns
Stay afloat

The Lighthouse
Standing
On the hill
The Lighthouse
Beaming
Out God's Will

Brightest Light
So much joy
Fill my vessel
Land ahoy

My Lighthouse
Standing
On the hill
My Lighthouse
Beaming
Out God's Will

Trust

Trust in life – a perfect shape
Trust in time – it will escape
Trust in you. Climbing walls
Trust in me. Catching falls

Elements lie on the grass
Shatter me like broken glass
Kind words gather on the ground
Pieces gently lost and found

Surrender now
Beneath the clock
God will strike
Courageous knock

Pleasures, treasures, all await
Echoes of an endless fate
See the door – it's just ajar
Doves of freedom fly from far

Falling rays of brilliant sun
Warming comfort, slow down One.
Listen softly, happy parts,
Arms surround – Life is an Art.

Trust the castle that you find
Safety for a furrowed mind
Intense relief rests inside
Trusting loving God will guide.

Imperfect Pitch

What is that space between us called?
Such yearning for it to unfold!
It's as a wall! He won't come in.
Though every night I dream of him.

His every word, a drop of gold,
Every look, into my soul,
The words and thoughts I long to share,
Questions. Answers. Leave me bare.
The beauty of his every thought,
Draws me deep. Powerless. Caught.

Waiting for that resonation
To take us to our destination.

Gone

Your towel
Still hangs,
On the bedroom door
Hug it tight…
Breathe you into my core

Your pillow
Unchanged,
Rests still on 'your side'.
Hold it close…
Tears warm my eyes

Your notes
Still rest, beside my bed
(Words from the past will hurt my head)

My thoughts
Still rack-up every day
All I want to share and say

My love
Still lingers. On and on.
Praying that you haven't gone.

Insecurity

Sad. Wondering.
Thoughts wandering.
Much worrying.
Thoughts pondering.

You're in my heart.
You're in my past.
I really thought
That it would last.

The almighty stop.
Shattered that.
I feel bereft –
I want you back.

Back to those times:
Secure and laughter,
Looking forward
To our happy after.

And now, it seems all confused.
New rules replace our happy muse.

My broken heart
Can't deal with 'finish',

But you want change,
And I'm barely in it.

And, what are you now?
A friend or more?
I dare not ask.
Just want 'before'.

But how once it was,
It is no more.
The change has come.
Life: insecure.

The curiousity of never knowing

A part of me
Wants to share
Feelings which
Should not be there

So wrong
No need
To knock him from
His solid steed

An applecart
Already sweet
Happy couple
Rows so neat.

And yet his words
Stir up feelings
So desiring
A body reeling

And 'neath the flesh
A simple call
Of innocence
To know it all

To dream of youth
And know 'what if'
Way back then...
A simple kiss
Would change it all
Would set us growing
Oh, the curiosity
Of never knowing!

Always knowing

Curiosity
A feline horror
A parallel life
So wrong to borrow

In vivid thoughts
All the wonder
Of what and how
A mind to plunder

Just to know
How soft those lips
Gentle, touch..
Fingertips.

A fever pitch
Inside my house
Hands, legs, flesh
Caressing mouth.

And peaceful moments
Within warm arms
Eyes closed, relaxed
And safely charmed.

Soft grass, birds sing,
Sun lights their tree.
Two souls of nature
Wings open: free!

These thoughts a dream, though,
Only fleeting
Because there is
No way of meeting.

Shut down! Shut up!
Pure fantasy:
His hands will never
Run up me.

Morals, turmoils
Others' hearts.
All are keeping
Us apart.

Locked down, locked out
Yet feelings growing.
To never know,
But always knowing.

Thawed Thoughts

It started as a tiny drop
Rolling down the word forgot

The World has fallen upside down
The Ice Maiden has lost her crown
Her lofty highs, are now a-flow
Sun-fractured dreams slip below

Cold splinters of a precious past
Turned to slush - it went so fast
Water pooling in her eyes
Blurring all she sees inside

Clutching at the shrinking pieces
But warm hands melt, and form decreases!
Fragments of some other times
Mismatched in her leaking mind

Thawing memoirs, looking back,
Oblivious to Spring's attack
Hopeful breakthroughs soon diminish
Ice-white matter a watery finish

Her essence now is all that's left
Pretty in a summer dress
Winter just a distant memory
Season closed. Vessel empty.

Working from home

Washing up looks appealing
Dirty dishes may coax the feeling
Marigolds sink beneath bubbles
Seeking refuge, finding trouble
Knives and forks pricking conscience
Come on now it's your last chance!
Dishes draining
Confidence waning
Motivation muster...
Distracted by duster!
Disco now with the hoover
Who would know, I'm quite the mover?!
Energised: plug in laptop
Ding! Ding! Filling up inbox
Give it an hour -
Oh, lost will power
23 emails - that's enough
Does anyone ever read this stuff?
Max effort exhausted me
Think I'd better make some tea.

Awaiting Grace

Procrastination:
A vicar's dinner
Hunger burns
Inside the sinners

Insulated Truth

Lives his life as a Thermos flask:
Robust exterior hides shameful past
His inner world, so easily broken
Won't believe a bright word spoken.

Smiles and stories serve to hide
Dark secrets poured down, deep inside.
Black teabags loom, the size of mountains
Mock painful thoughts - silenced by drowning

But amber wisps are leaking out
Change of topic! Plug the spout!
Screw down stopper just in time
Seal up spirals of his mind

Unsavoury elixir safely hidden
Doubly insulated into submission
A vacuumed relief marks this day,
As his new journey gets underway.

But Noon arrives and makes him sweat
A thirst transpires, an appetite whet.
Her midday warmth should offer solace
But panic! No! He loses courage.

The knowledge of what's been before
He fears will only close her door.
His lips are dry and sorely parched
Why must his secrets stay so dark?

This man afraid to open his challis
Believes it would unscrew great malice.
But dare he risk a stolen taste,
When there's no clouds to hide her face?

She will see, and he'll regret
Shameful tales he can't forget
But does he only make presumption?
Could she offer him redemption?

Her sunshine arms brush his brow
And gradually he wonders how
To insulate her from the truth
And keep his self-esteem aloof?

But dehydration's getting stronger
Remedy can wait no longer
And now the flask is in his hands
Praying that she'll understand.

Once lid is off, no turning back
Hiss of relief as it opens a crack
He turns his shamed-face to the Sun
Believing that his time has come.

Would she like a cup of sorrow?
(Will his Sun set on tomorrow?)
Reluctantly, he pours two measures
A sinking heart, sapped of pleasures.

His whirling mind expecting wrestles,
Watching as she takes her vessel
Will this ceremony be their last?
A lamentation of the past?

A nervous sigh, as she begins,
To share and sip his long-carried sins.
Anticipating winces as cup meets lips
Expecting revulsion at bitter tea sips

But no! She says, it's like a tonic!
Noone can possibly be bionic!
Her face is beaming,
His truth is gleaming!

So happy that his warmth escaped
She's very glad he isn't fake.
And now their cups are overflowing
A future bright at the knowing

A Special Reality

The birth was wondrous – such an event!
Visitors, joy, great intent!

The doctors came: a diagnosis
Something wrong…bleak prognosis

Still the faith lingered there
Precious hopes hung in the air

No let up. A constant watch
Abandon friends: I just could not.

Years drift by. Sleepless nights.
Like a toddler. Anguish. Fights.

"When will he…?" " You're so strong!"
"I DON'T KNOW!" "I CAN'T GO ON!"

Grieving life, cut lose dreams
Reality is never as it seems

Fix You

Eyes shut upon your pillow
I dream of a different fellow
Able, chatty, ease of life
Always staying out of strife

Midnight sitting at the kitchen table
Researching ways to make you able
What is out there that will fix you?
Eyes still searching as clock hits a dark two.

Five thirty AM on the dot
Wailing seizures in your cot
Groundhog Day begins again
Every week feels the same.

Midnight sitting at the kitchen table
Researching ways to make you able
What is out there that will fix you?
Eyes still searching as clock hits a dark two.

Adrenaline wake-up starts the day
Surely there must be a way
To find a normal once again
With no tiredness to mask the pain

Midnight sitting at the kitchen table
Researching ways to make you able
What is out there that will fix you?
Eyes still searching as clock hits a dark two.

Your real alarm begins my shift
Your blue eyes wanting more than this
Automated dedication
Never consider resignation!

Midnight sitting at the kitchen table
Researching ways to make you able
Suddenly, the reading's worth it:
Therapies which seem a sure fit!

Training, learning, put it into practice
Come on my sweet boy, we can crack this!
Weeks go by: a new routine
Wait - is this a change I've seen?!

Yes, it IS! We jump for joy!
Look how he can use that toy!
Now we know this, must keep going
For where it will end, there's no knowing!

Breakfast sitting at the kitchen table
Another test to monitor if you're able
More tasks designed to try and fix you
Keep on going 'til clock hits afternoon two.

Every day now, seeing progress
Feeling happy that I know this!
Each day, tasks go on and on
But where has your 'mummy' gone?

Midnight sitting at the kitchen table
Research more ways to make you able
What more is out there that will fix you?
Eyes still searching as clock hits a dark two.

Another milestone, another rung!
But when will we ever say we're done?
Look around – this life's still tough!
Look at your son…he's done enough!

Midnight sitting at the kitchen table
Celebrating the ways we made you able
Love and laughter replace 'try to fix you'
All eyes sleeping as clock hits a dark two.

Hold on, Let go

Hold on
Breathe in
Relax
Breathe Out
Let go

Hold on
Relax
Let Go

Breathe in
Breathe out

Hold on
Let go

Hold on to smiles
Hold on to kindness
Hold on to compassion
Hold on to blessings

Hold on to being alive
Hold on to gratitude
Hold on to thanks
Hold on to connection

Hold on to forgiveness
Hold on to positivity
Hold on to calm
Hold on to peace

Hold on to laughter
Hold onto light
Hold onto energy
Hold onto eternity

Hold onto love

Let go of tension
Let go of tiredness
Let go of all wants
Let go of all attachments

Let go of anger
Let go of memories
Let go of judgement
Let go of all expectations

Let go of all worries
Let go of responsibilities
Let go of noise
Let go of all feelings

Let go of the past
Let go of now
Let go of the future
Let go of time

Let go of holding on

Breathe in
Breathe out

Hold on
Let go

Reverse Time

Hold on,
this planet's so precious we need to
recognise that
there's only one chance. But do we?
We think we can
reverse time,
but we cannot
just count down
and
let go

They say,

"Let go
and
just count down"
But we cannot reverse time.
We think we can.
There's only one chance. But do we
recognise that
this planet's so precious we need to
hold on?!

Gravity of Life

Is all life predetermined?
Or are we free to choose?
Demands for binary answers
Serve only to confuse.

The answers lie in nature,
Visuals from the land
All the information
To help us understand.

Spruce-sprinkled mountain,
River source on top.
Your life journey begins here,
In a sparkling, dewy drop.

From icy spring to bubbling stream,
Your river twists and cuts its path
Countless drops of experience
From turbulent to smooth as glass.

And there you sit
Upon this flow
In your kayak
Down you go.

Free to choose
Which course to take,
Free to choose
To speed or brake.

Steer your craft with your paddle
Your choice to stop for views
Enticing you with sweetness
An intoxicating cruise.

Leaving speed for tomorrow
Hope it's not too late
Lazy days of summer
Before they open any gates.

Drifting on your mill pond
Life slowly floating by
But tides they will find you
Boat on a downward slide.

A flood's sudden arrival
Gashes banks and stirs up land
Quick – an epiphany!
You must take your blade in hand.

This life's your one and only
And your best way you must steer
Past rocks and roots and rapids
Because your purpose is now clear!

Your guiding river is unwinding
Sometimes smooth, sometimes rough.
Occasionally, you take passengers
For the happy times and the tough.

You're understanding life now
It's a wisdom you must voice:
Possibilities predetermined
But you always have a choice.

So then begs the question,
Of the Force which pulls you down?
Ceaseless, never-ending
A mystifying Noun.

There is a certainty we all know
That the river has an end.
An estuary of life into ocean
Into which we all will blend.

And as you take your final stroke
The waters become clear
You see everything connecting
The Truth without veneer:

Gravity was your Purpose
Guiding you though life
Hidden from your vision
Yet clues there always in sight.

Ingram Content Group UK Ltd.
Milton Keynes UK
UKHW021028300323
419408UK00016B/1106

9 789357 617451